FM 30-34

BASIC FIELD MANUAL

MILITARY INTELLIGENCE
IDENTIFICATION OF SOVIET-RUSSIAN AIRCRAFT

Prepared under direction of the
Chief of Staff

UNITED STATES
GOVERNMENT PRINTING OFFICE
WASHINGTON : 1941

WAR DEPARTMENT,
WASHINGTON, July 18, 1941.

FM 30-34, Military Intelligence, Identification of Soviet-Russian Aircraft, is published for the information and guidance of all concerned.

[A. G. 062.11 (6-5-41).]

BY ORDER OF THE SECRETARY OF WAR:

G. C. MARSHALL,
Chief of Staff.

OFFICIAL:
E. S. ADAMS,
Major General,
The Adjutant General.

FM 30-34

BASIC FIELD MANUAL

MILITARY INTELLIGENCE

IDENTIFICATION OF SOVIET-RUSSIAN AIRCRAFT

The material contained in this manual has been secured from many sources. It is the best material available but may be incomplete and, in some respects, inaccurate.

This manual containing illustrations with explanatory data relative to Soviet-Russian aircraft is published for limited distribution. It will be used for instruction of officers and men in appearance and general characteristics of Soviet-Russian aircraft and will be safeguarded as prescribed in AR 380-5.

This tabulation does not include airplanes taken over from the former Baltic States, Lithuania, Estonia, and Latvia.

Soviet-Russian airplane markings consist of red stars as shown below:

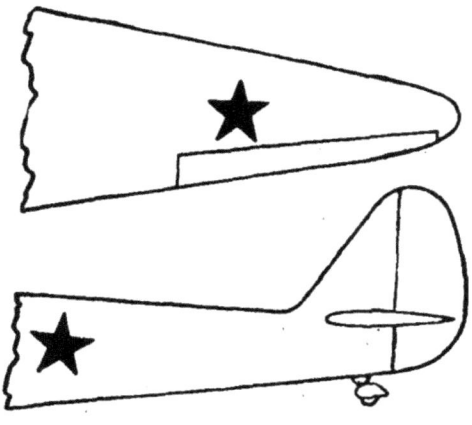

MILITARY AIRCRAFT

IDENTIFICATION OF SOVIET-RUSSIAN AIRCRAFT

RUSSIAN
ARMY

Pursuit I-15

Straight, round tip, open cockpit, single motor, fixed landing gear, biplane. Later models have retractable landing gear. Resembles Boeing P 12 E.

Crew:	One.
Armament:	Four 7.62 machine guns, fixed.
Ammunition:	3,000 rounds total.
Bomb load:	110 pounds.
Radio:	
Armor:	5-mm plate back of pilot's seat.
Motors:	One M25 (B), 750 horsepower at 9,512 feet or M62, 830 horsepower at 4,592 feet or 800 horsepower at 13,776 feet.
Maximum speed:	235 miles per hour.
Rate of climb:	16,400 feet in 6½ minutes.
Service ceiling:	26,000 to 29,500 feet.
Maximum range:	408 miles or 2½ hours, endurance.
Wing span:	30 feet.

PURSUIT
I-15

IDENTIFICATION OF SOVIET-RUSSIAN AIRCRAFT

RUSSIAN
ARMY

PURSUIT I–16

Straight leading edge, round tip, slightly tapered, low-wing monoplane, inclosed cockpit, square nose, retractable landing gear (ski or wheels).

Crew:	One.
Armament:	Four 7.62 machine guns fixed or two machine guns fixed and two cannon.
Ammunition:	
Bomb load:	
Radio:	
Armor:	8-mm plate back of cockpit.
Motors:	One M25 (B), 750 horsepower at 27,512 feet (Wright Cyclone) or one M62, 850 horsepower at 4,600 feet or 800 horsepower at 13,776 feet.
Maximum speed:	280 miles per hour.
Rate of climb:	16,400 feet in 6½ minutes.
Service ceiling:	31,500 feet.
Maximum range:	400 miles or 1.5 hours in flight.
Wing span:	29 feet.

PURSUIT
I-16

With skis and Finnish markings.

IDENTIFICATION OF SOVIET-RUSSIAN AIRCRAFT

RUSSIAN
ARMY

PURSUIT I-17 (TSKB-19; ZKB-19)

Slightly swept-back, round tip, slightly tapered, low-wing, single motor, monoplane, long pointed nose, fixed landing gear, probably available only in small numbers (40 on hand January 24, 1941).

Crew:	One.
Armament:	Two to four fixed machine guns; 1 cannon 20-mm.
Ammunition:	
Bomb load:	
Radio:	
Armor:	Plating behind pilot seat.
Motors:	One M100, 860 horsepower at 11,808 feet (Hispano-Suiza) 12 y.
Maximum speed:	307 miles per hour at 13,120 feet.
Rate of climb:	12,870 feet in 5 minutes 12 seconds.
Service ceiling:	32,800 feet.
Maximum range:	532 miles or 2½ hours.
Wing span:	33 feet.

IDENTIFICATION OF SOVIET-RUSSIAN AIRCRAFT

PURSUIT I-17
(TSKB-19; ZKB-19)

IDENTIFICATION OF SOVIET-RUSSIAN AIRCRAFT

RUSSIAN
ARMY

PURSUIT DI-4 (TWO-SEAT FIGHTER)

Two-seat biplane. Obsolescent.

Crew: Two.
Armament: Three fixed and one flexible machine gun.
Ammunition:
Bomb load: 220 pounds.
Radio:
Armor:
Motors: One 680 horsepower M17 (BMW VI).
Maximum speed: 180 miles per hour.
Rate of climb: 16,400 feet in 13 minutes.
Service ceiling: 19,680 feet.
Maximum range: 325 miles.
Wing span:

IDENTIFICATION OF SOVIET-RUSSIAN AIRCRAFT

PURSUIT DI-4
(TWO-SEAT
FIGHTER)

IDENTIFICATION OF SOVIET-RUSSIAN AIRCRAFT

RUSSIAN ARMY

PURSUIT DI-6

Straight, round tip, inclosed cockpit, single motor biplane, with lower wing negative dihedral. Also used for ground attack.

Crew: Two.
Armament: Two fixed machine guns; one or two flexible machine guns.
Ammunition:
Bomb load:
Radio:
Armor:
Motors: One M25, 750 horsepower at 27,512 feet (Wright Cyclone).
Maximum speed: 224 miles per hour at 9,840 feet.
Rate of climb:
Service ceiling: 31,800 feet.
Maximum range: 500 miles or 3 hours.
Wing span:

IDENTIFICATION OF SOVIET-RUSSIAN AIRCRAFT

PURSUIT
DI-6

IDENTIFICATION OF SOVIET-RUSSIAN AIRCRAFT

RUSSIAN
ARMY

PURSUIT-SEVERSKY, P-35 (N. V.)

Straight front edge, rounded trailing edge, low-wing monoplane, all metal, single motor, inclosed cockpit, retractable landing gear, noticeable bulge when wheels are retracted, also finished as double-seater pursuit plane, convoy work.

Crew:	Two.
Armament:	Two fixed machine guns.
Ammunition:	
Bomb load:	
Radio:	
Armor:	
Motors:	One Pratt & Whitney "Twin Wasp," 950 horsepower at 14,100 feet.
Maximum speed:	285 miles per hour at 14,100 feet.
Rate of climb:	13,120 feet in 5 minutes.
Service ceiling:	29,500 feet.
Maximum range:	438 miles or 2 hours.
Wing span:	

PURSUIT–SEVERSKY
P–35 (N. V.)

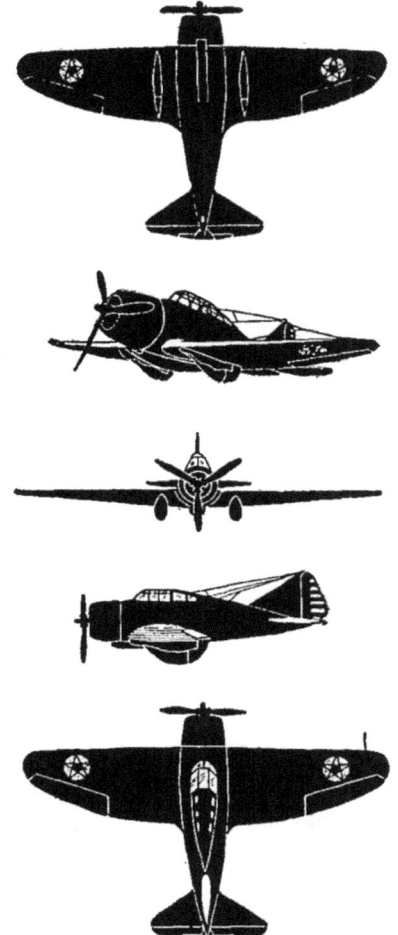

Finished as double-seater pursuit plane (convoy).

IDENTIFICATION OF SOVIET-RUSSIAN AIRCRAFT

RUSSIAN
ARMY

FIGHTER I-7

Biplane—an obsolescent type.

Crew:	One.
Armament:	Four machine guns.
Ammunition:	
Bomb load:	
Radio:	
Armor:	
Motors:	One 600 horsepower M17 (BMW VI).
Maximum speed:	210 miles per hour.
Rate of climb:	9,840 feet in 3.8 minutes.
Service ceiling:	29,500 feet.
Maximum range:	372 miles.
Wing span:	

IDENTIFICATION OF SOVIET-RUSSIAN AIRCRAFT

FIGHTER
I-7

IDENTIFICATION OF SOVIET-RUSSIAN AIRCRAFT

RUSSIAN ARMY

FIGHTER I-18

Crew:
Armament:
Ammunition:
Bomb load:
Radio:
Armor:
Motors: One 1,150 horsepower, M105.
Maximum speed: 372 miles per hour.
Rate of climb:
Service ceiling:
Maximum range: 2½ hours.
Wing span:

IDENTIFICATION OF SOVIET-RUSSIAN AIRCRAFT

FIGHTER
I-18

IDENTIFICATION OF SOVIET-RUSSIAN AIRCRAFT

RUSSIAN ARMY

GROUND ATTACK LR

Two-seat biplane. Similar to RZ reconnaissance plane—an obsolescent type.

Crew: Two.
Armament:
Ammunition:
Bomb load:
Radio:
Armor:
Motors: One 830 horsepower M34 (perhaps two motors in wing).
Maximum speed: 186 miles per hour.
Rate of climb:
Service ceiling:
Maximum range:
Wing span:

IDENTIFICATION OF SOVIET-RUSSIAN AIRCRAFT

GROUND ATTACK
LR

IDENTIFICATION OF SOVIET-RUSSIAN AIRCRAFT

RUSSIAN ARMY

MEDIUM BOMBER ZKB-26

Twin-engined, all metal, midwing monoplane, inclosed cabin, retractable landing gear.

Crew:
Armament:
Ammunition:
Bomb load:
Radio:
Armor:
Motors: Two M85, 800 horsepower.
Maximum speed: 220 miles per hour.
Rate of climb:
Service ceiling:
Maximum range:
Wing span:

IDENTIFICATION OF SOVIET-RUSSIAN AIRCRAFT

MEDIUM BOMBER
ZKB-26

IDENTIFICATION OF SOVIET-RUSSIAN AIRCRAFT

RUSSIAN ARMY

BOMBER SB-1

Slightly dihedral, slightly swept-back, slightly tapered, round tip, midwing monoplane, two-motor, cabin, long blunt nose, fixed landing gear.

Crew:	Three.
Armament:	Three flexible machine guns.
Ammunition:	
Bomb load:	1,320 pounds, normal; 2,200 pounds, maximum.
Radio:	
Armor:	
Motors:	Two M25, 750 horsepower at 9,512 feet (Wright Cyclone).
Maximum speed:	272 miles at 9,840 feet.
Rate of climb:	16,400 feet in 9 minutes.
Service ceiling:	27,900 feet.
Maximum range:	500 miles, normal; 1,000 miles, maximum.
Wing span:	70 feet.

IDENTIFICATION OF SOVIET-RUSSIAN AIRCRAFT

BOMBER
SB-1

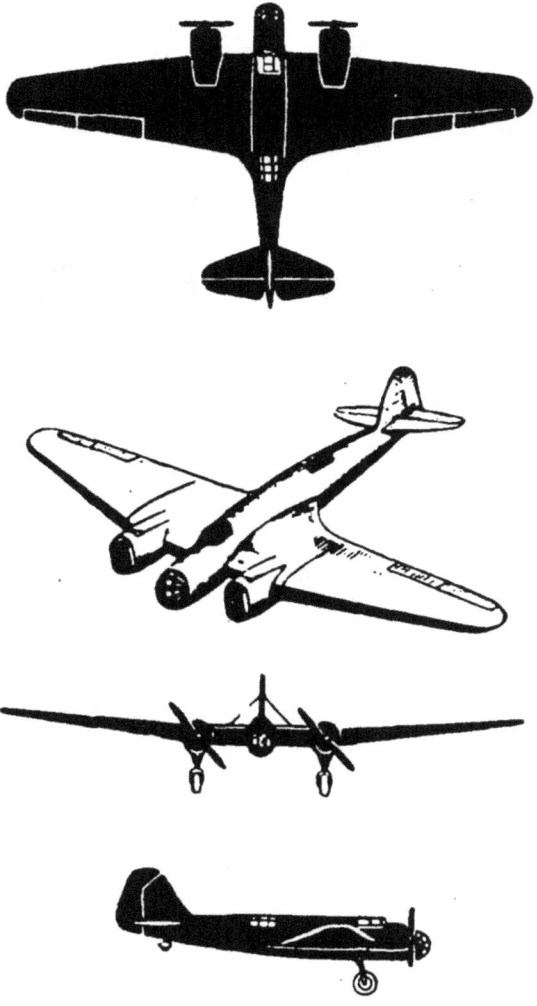

IDENTIFICATION OF SOVIET-RUSSIAN AIRCRAFT

RUSSIAN ARMY

BOMBER SB–2 (A. N. T. 40)

Slightly dihedral, slightly swept-back, slightly tapered, round tip, midwing monoplane, two-motor, cabin, long blunt nose, retractable landing gear or skis.

Crew:	Six.
Armament:	B Shkaas machine gun; one double barrel in nose; one to rear; one below.
Ammunition:	
Bomb load:	1,100 to 1,300 pounds.
Radio:	
Armor:	5-mm plate under and behind pilot's seat. Rubber covered fuel tanks.
Motors:	Two M100, 860 to 950 horsepower (Hispano-Suiza).
Maximum speed:	249 miles per hour at 13,120 feet.
Rate of climb:	16,400 feet in 9 minutes.
Service ceiling:	28,000 feet.
Maximum range:	600 to 750 miles.
Wing span:	66 feet.

BOMBER SB-2
(A. N. T. 40)

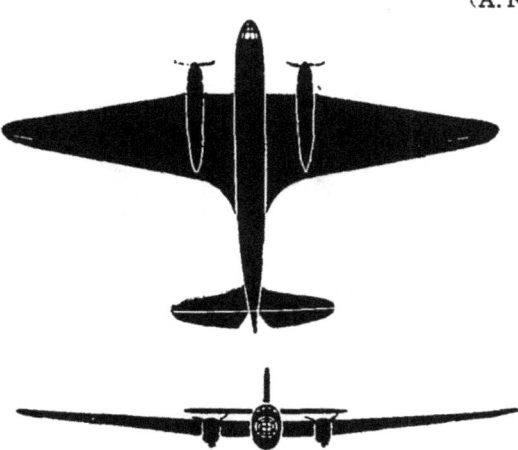

Finished with skis—nonretractable landing gears.

IDENTIFICATION OF SOVIET-RUSSIAN AIRCRAFT

RUSSIAN ARMY

With old Finnish markings.

BOMBER SB-3

Slightly dihedral, slightly swept-back, slightly tapered, round tip, midwing monoplane, two-motor, cabin, long blunt nose, retractable landing gear or skis.

Crew: Three or four.
Armament: Four flexible machine guns—two in nose, one in tail, one below.
Ammunition: 1,900 rounds for two; 1,050 rounds for tail gun; 700 rounds for belly gun.
Bomb load: 1,320 pounds, normal; 2,200 pounds, maximum.
Radio:
Armor:
Motors: Two M103, 860 horsepower at 14,000 feet (or two M105, 960 horsepower at 14,000 feet).
Maximum speed: 260 miles per hour.
Rate of climb: 16,400 feet in 9 minutes.
Service ceiling: 26,250 feet.
Maximum range: 500 miles, normal; 1,000 miles, maximum.
Wing span:

IDENTIFICATION OF SOVIET-RUSSIAN AIRCRAFT

BOMBER
SB-3

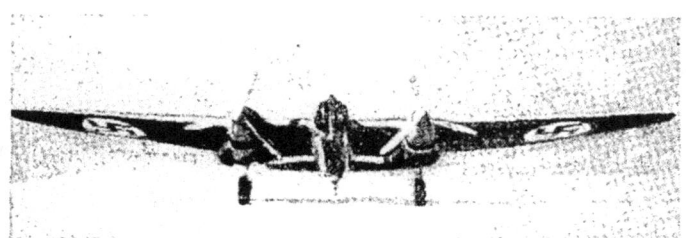

RUSSIAN ARMY

BOMBER DB-3 (ZKB-26)

Slightly dihedral, slightly swept-back, round tip, slightly tapered, midwing, cabin monoplane, two-motor, long rounded nose, retractable landing gear or skis.

Crew:	Three or four.
Armament:	Three flexible 7.62 machine guns (latest report four or five).
Ammunition:	1,100 rounds for four machine guns; 650 for other.
Bomb load:	2,200 pounds, normal.
Radio:	
Armor:	8-mm plate behind pilot.
Motors:	Two M87B, 850 to 950 horsepower at 15,416 feet (Gnome Rhone 14K).
Maximum speed:	269 miles per hour at 16,400 feet.
Rate of climb:	6,560 feet in 5 minutes or 13,120 feet in 12 minutes.
Service ceiling:	28,000 feet.
Maximum range:	1,750 to 2,000 miles.
Wing span:	70 feet.

IDENTIFICATION OF SOVIET-RUSSIAN AIRCRAFT

BOMBER DB-3
(ZKB-26)

IDENTIFICATION OF SOVIET-RUSSIAN AIRCRAFT

RUSSIAN
ARMY

BOMBER TB-5

Crew: Seven.
Armament: One cannon; five or six machine guns.
Ammunition:
Bomb load: 4,400 pounds.
Radio:
Armor:
Motors: Four.
Maximum speed: 155 miles per hour.
Rate of climb:
Service ceiling:
Maximum range: 8 to 10 hours.
Wing span:

IDENTIFICATION OF SOVIET-RUSSIAN AIRCRAFT

BOMBER
TB-5

**RUSSIAN
ARMY**

BOMBER TB-6 (A. N. T. 41)

Four-engine monoplane, heavy bomber.

Crew: Seven.
Armament: One fixed; five flexible machine guns.
Ammunition:
Bomb load: 4,410 to 6,600 pounds.
Radio:
Armor:
Motors: Four 830 horsepower supercharged.
Maximum speed: 310 miles per hour.
Rate of climb:
Service ceiling:
Maximum range: 10 hours endurance.
Wing span:

IDENTIFICATION OF SOVIET-RUSSIAN AIRCRAFT

BOMBER TB-6
(A. N. T. 41)

IDENTIFICATION OF SOVIET-RUSSIAN AIRCRAFT

RUSSIAN
ARMY

BOMBER TB-7

Slightly swept-back, slightly tapered, round tip, cabin, four-motor monoplane, decidedly long pointed nose, retractable landing gear. Might be found only in experimental series.

Crew:	Seven or nine.
Armament:	Three flexible machine guns; two flexible cannon.
Ammunition:	
Bomb load:	5,500 pounds.
Radio:	
Armor:	
Motors:	Four AM34, 1,000 horsepower, and one M100 (driven by means of charger) 860 horsepower at 11,808 feet.

Maximum speed: 250 miles at 16,400 feet.
Rate of climb:
Service ceiling:
Maximum range: 2,000 miles.
Wing span:

IDENTIFICATION OF SOVIET-RUSSIAN AIRCRAFT

**BOMBER
TB-7**

RUSSIAN
ARMY

BOMBER, VULTEE V-11 (LB Sch ?)

Straight, round tip, low-wing monoplane, all metal, single motor, inclosed cockpit, long blunt nose, retractable landing gear, used as light bomber and ground attack airplane.

Crew:	Two or three.
Armament:	Six fixed machine guns; one or two flexible.
Ammunition:	
Bomb load:	594 pounds, normal; 1,320 pounds, maximum.
Radio:	
Armor:	
Motors:	One Wright Cyclone, SGR-1820-G2, 850 horsepower at 5,904 feet.
Maximum speed:	238 miles at 6,560 feet.
Rate of climb:	13,120 feet in 13 minutes.
Service ceiling:	24,300 feet.
Maximum range:	1,062 miles, normal; 2,000 miles, maximum.
Wing span:	50 feet.

BOMBER
VULTEE V-11
LB SCH

RUSSIAN
ARMY

DIVE BOMBER I-153

"CHICKA"

Straight, round tip, open cockpit, single-motor biplane, retractable landing gear.

Crew:	One.
Armament:	Four 7.62-mm Shkaas machine guns.
Ammunition:	
Bomb load:	330 pounds.
Radio:	
Armor:	8-mm plate back of seat.
Motors:	One M62 (Wright Cyclone); 830 to 1,000 horsepower.
Maximum speed:	245 miles per hour (approximate).
Rate of climb:	
Service ceiling:	32,800 feet.
Maximum range:	238 miles (1.1 hours).
Wing span:	33 feet.

DIVE BOMBER
I-153
"CHICKA"

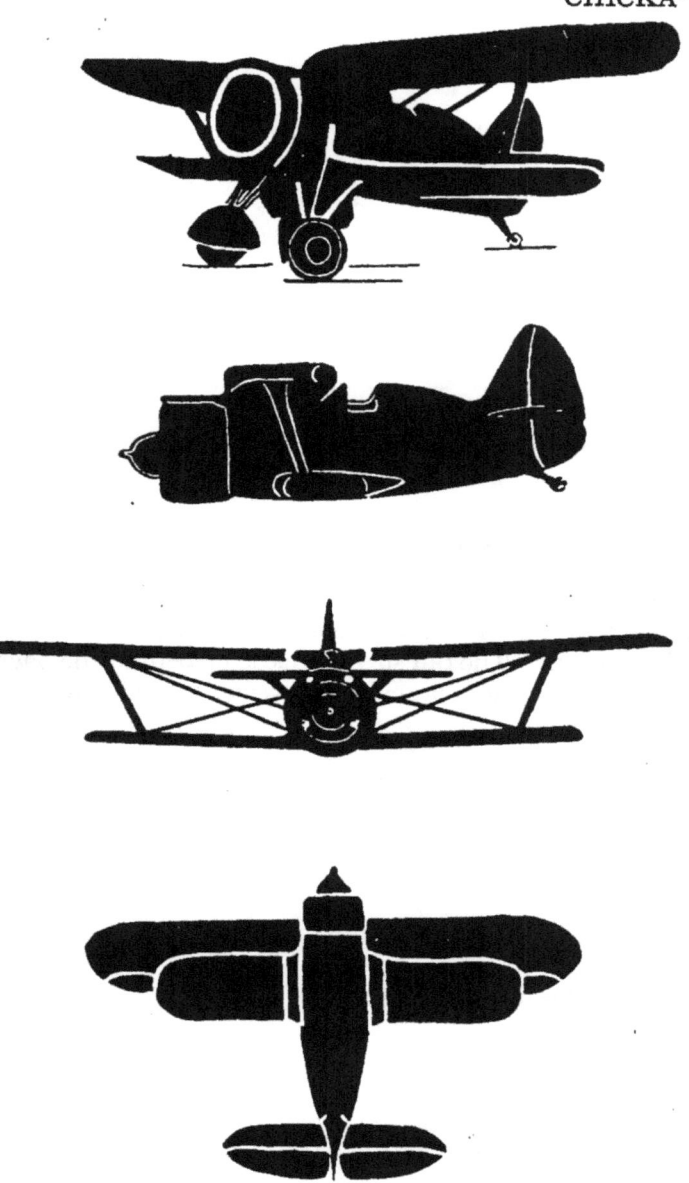

RUSSIAN
ARMY

EXPERIMENTAL BOMBER OR FIGHTER TYPE

Two-motor, high-wing monoplane without fuselage. Flippers are high up on vertical stabilizer. Wing section between motors is clear. The tail surfaces close up behind the nacelles. Center wing section probably does not extend back to tail surfaces.

Crew: Two or three.
Armament:
Ammunition:
Bomb load:
Radio:
Armor:
Motors:
Maximum speed: Appears fast.
Rate of climb:
Service ceiling:
Maximum range:
Wing span:

IDENTIFICATION OF SOVIET-RUSSIAN AIRCRAFT

EXPERIMENTAL BOMBER OR FIGHTER TYPE

IDENTIFICATION OF SOVIET-RUSSIAN AIRCRAFT

RUSSIAN
ARMY

LIGHT BOMBER GV-25 (EXPERIMENTAL)

Crew:
Armament:
Ammunition:
Bomb load:
Radio:
Armor:
Motors:
Maximum speed:
Rate of climb:
Service ceiling:
Maximum range:
Wing span:

IDENTIFICATION OF SOVIET-RUSSIAN AIRCRAFT

LIGHT BOMBER
GV-25
(EXPERIMENTAL)

RUSSIAN
ARMY

RECONNAISSANCE BOMBER (EXPERIMENTAL)

Slightly swept-back, round tip, tapered, two midwing motors, midwing monoplane. Diamond-shaped tail plane with twin rudder fins. Fairly long slim tapered nose on same line with engine nacelles (still in experimental stage).

Crew:
Armament:
Ammunition:
Bomb load: 660 pounds.
Radio:
Armor:
Motors: Two.
Maximum speed:
Rate of climb:
Service ceiling:
Maximum range: 1,200 miles.
Wing span:

IDENTIFICATION OF SOVIET-RUSSIAN AIRCRAFT

RECONNAISSANCE BOMBER
(EXPERIMENTAL)

RUSSIAN
ARMY

LONG RANGE BOMBER (T. S. K. B. 26)

Slightly swept-back, slightly tapered, round tip, low-wing monoplane, closed cockpit, two motors, retractable landing gear.

Crew:
Armament:
Ammunition:
Bomb load:
Radio:
Armor:
Motors:
Maximum speed:
Rate of climb:
Service ceiling:
Maximum range:
Wing span:

IDENTIFICATION OF SOVIET-RUSSIAN AIRCRAFT

LONG RANGE BOMBER
(T. S. K. B. 26)

IDENTIFICATION OF SOVIET-RUSSIAN AIRCRAFT

RUSSIAN
ARMY

ARMY COOPERATION AND STORM S. S. S.

Straight, round tip, biplane, closed cockpit, fixed landing gear.

Crew:
Armament:
Ammunition:
Bomb load:
Radio:
Armor:
Motors:
Maximum speed:
Rate of climb:
Service ceiling:
Maximum range:
Wing span: 51 feet.

IDENTIFICATION OF SOVIET-RUSSIAN AIRCRAFT

ARMY COOPERATION AND STORM
S. S. S.

RUSSIAN
ARMY

RECONNAISSANCE R-3

Two-seat, all metal sesquiplane. Obsolescent type.

Crew: Two.
Armament: One fixed and one flexible machine gun.
Ammunition:
Bomb load: 440 pounds.
Radio:
Armor:
Motors: One 480 horsepower M22 (Gnome-Rhone Jupiter).
Maximum speed: 112 miles per hour.
Rate of climb: 16,400 feet in 50 minutes.
Service ceiling: 19,350 feet.
Maximum range: 435 miles.
Wing span:

RECONNAISSANCE
R-3

IDENTIFICATION OF SOVIET-RUSSIAN AIRCRAFT

RUSSIAN
ARMY

RECONNAISSANCE R-5

Straight, round tip, biplane, single motor, open cockpit, fixed landing gear, reconnaissance plane. Still used as dispatch carrier and practice plane. Obsolescent type.

Crew:	Two.
Armament:	Two machine guns; one flexible, one fixed.
Ammunition:	680 rounds for flexible; 425 rounds for fixed machine gun.
Bomb load:	560 pounds.
Radio:	
Armor:	
Motors:	One M17, 600 horsepower at 328 feet.
Maximum speed:	132 miles per hour.
Rate of climb:	16,000 feet in 24 minutes.
Service ceiling:	22,000 feet.
Maximum range:	620 miles without bombs.
Wing span:	50 feet.

IDENTIFICATION OF SOVIET-RUSSIAN AIRCRAFT

RECONNAISSANCE
R-5

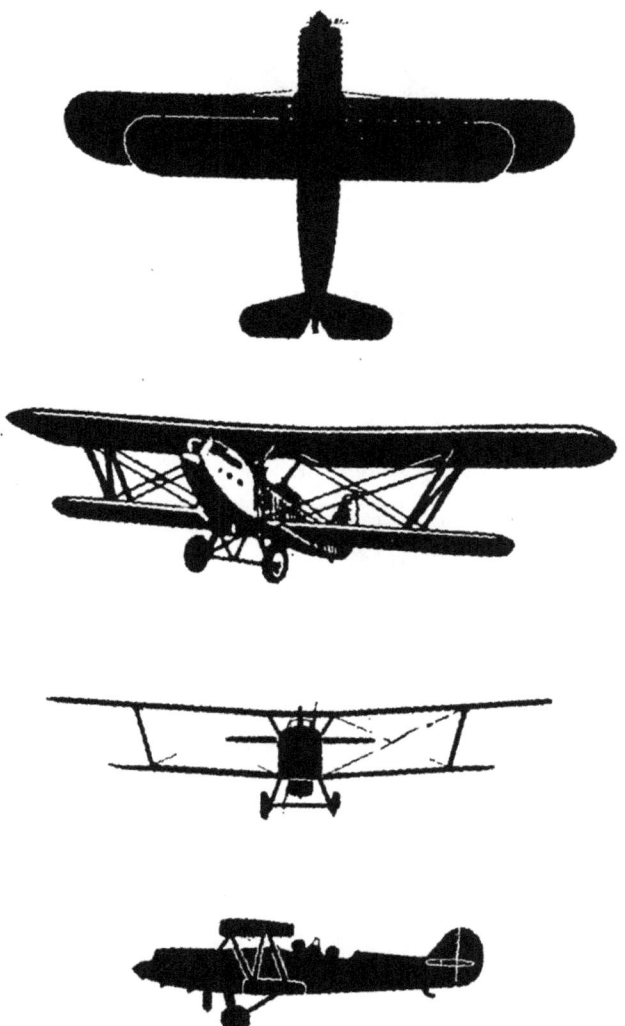

IDENTIFICATION OF SOVIET-RUSSIAN AIRCRAFT

RUSSIAN
ARMY

RECONNAISSANCE R-6

Straight, square tip, low-wing monoplane, fixed landing gear, antiquated reconnaissance plane now used as practice and transport airplane.

Crew:	Three or four.
Armament:	Three flexible.
Ammunition:	
Bomb load:	1,100 pounds.
Radio:	
Armor:	
Motors:	Two M17, 600 horsepower at 328 feet or two M34, 850 horsepower at 6,560 feet.
Maximum speed:	169 miles per hour at 6,560 feet.
Rate of climb:	14,200 feet in 16 minutes.
Service ceiling:	21,300 feet.
Maximum range:	1,250 miles without bombs.
Wing span:	41 feet.

IDENTIFICATION OF SOVIET-RUSSIAN AIRCRAFT

RECONNAISSANCE
R-6

IDENTIFICATION OF SOVIET-RUSSIAN AIRCRAFT

**RUSSIAN
ARMY**

RECONNAISSANCE R–7

Crew:
Armament:
Ammunition:
Bomb load:
Radio:
Armor:
Motors: One.
Maximum speed:
Rate of climb:
Service ceiling:
Maximum range:
Wing span:

RECONNAISSANCE
R-7

RUSSIAN
ARMY

RECONNAISSANCE R-10

Slightly dihedral, swept-back, straight trailing edge, single motor, cabin, blunt nose, low-wing monoplane, retractable landing gear.

Crew:	Two.
Armament:	Two machine guns, fixed; two flexible machine guns in turret.
Ammunition:	
Bomb load:	660 pounds.
Radio:	
Armor:	
Motors:	One (Wright Cyclone R-1820-F52, corresponds to M25) 760 horsepower at 5,904 feet.
Maximum speed:	217 miles per hour.
Rate of climb:	
Service ceiling:	24,928 feet.
Maximum range:	600 miles.
Wing span:	43 feet.

IDENTIFICATION OF SOVIET-RUSSIAN AIRCRAFT

RECONNAISSANCE
R-10

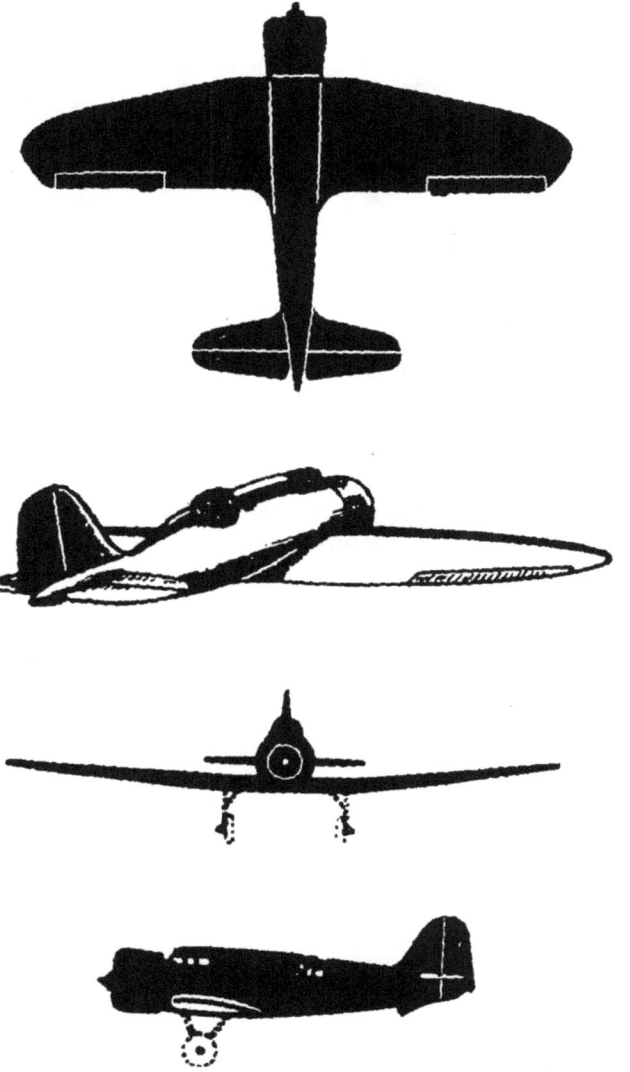

RUSSIAN ARMY

RECONNAISSANCE, R–Z

Reconnaissance plane, straight, round tip, biplane, single motor with fixed landing gear. Also used as light combat and ground attack plane. A development of the R–5 type.

Crew:	Two.
Armament:	Two fixed machine guns, one flexible machine gun.
Ammunition:	
Bomb load:	
Radio:	
Armor:	
Motors:	One M34, 850 horsepower at 6,560 feet.
Maximum speed:	181 miles at 6,560 feet.
Rate of climb:	16,400 feet in 15 minutes.
Service ceiling:	27,880 feet.
Maximum range:	500 miles without bombs.
Wing span:	

IDENTIFICATION OF SOVIET-RUSSIAN AIRCRAFT

RECONNAISSANCE
R-Z

IDENTIFICATION OF SOVIET-RUSSIAN AIRCRAFT

RUSSIAN
ARMY

OBSERVATION RD (A. N. T. 25) (LIGHT BOMBER)

Single-engined, long-range, low-wing monoplane with retractable landing gear.

Crew: Three.
Armament: Three machine guns; one cannon.
Ammunition:
Bomb load: 880 pounds.
Radio:
Armor:
Motors: One 940 horsepower M34 V-engine.
Maximum speed: 161 miles per hour.
Rate of climb:
Service ceiling:
Maximum range: 3,720 miles.
Wing span: 112 feet.

IDENTIFICATION OF SOVIET-RUSSIAN AIRCRAFT

OBSERVATION RD (A. N. T. 25)
(LIGHT BOMBER)

IDENTIFICATION OF SOVIET-RUSSIAN AIRCRAFT

RUSSIAN ARMY

TRANSPORT PS-84 (DOUGLAS DC-3)

Dihedral, swept-back, round tip, low-wing, cabin, monoplane, all metal, two-motor, retractable landing gear.

Crew: Three (crew), 21 passengers.
Armament:
Ammunition:
Bomb load:
Radio:
Armor:
Motors: Two Wright Cyclone SGR-1820-G2, 850 horsepower at 5,904 feet.
Maximum speed: 213 miles per hour at 6,560 feet.
Rate of climb: 10,000 feet in 9 minutes.
Service ceiling: 20,800 feet.
Maximum range: 875 miles, normal; 1,625 miles, maximum.
Wing span: 95 feet.

IDENTIFICATION OF SOVIET-RUSSIAN AIRCRAFT

TRANSPORT
PS-84
(DOUGLAS DC-3)

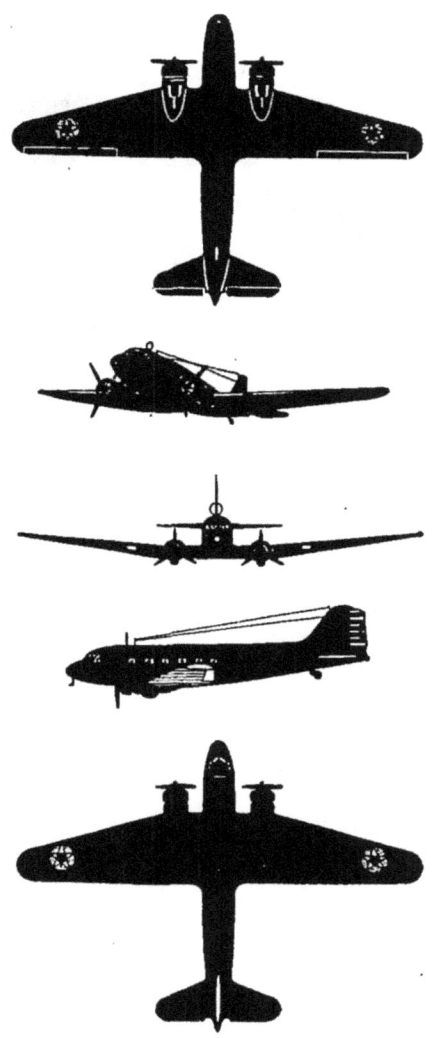

IDENTIFICATION OF SOVIET-RUSSIAN AIRCRAFT

RUSSIAN ARMY

TRANSPORT L-760

Slightly swept-back, slightly tapered, round tip, midwing monoplane, cabin, decidedly long pointed nose, fixed landing gear.

Crew: 10 (crew), 38 passengers.
Armament:
Ammunition:
Bomb load:
Radio:
Armor:
Motors: Six AM34, 1,200 horsepower.
Maximum speed: 188 miles at 6,560 feet.
Rate of climb:
Service ceiling: 22,960 feet.
Maximum range: 1,875 miles.
Wing span:

IDENTIFICATION OF SOVIET-RUSSIAN AIRCRAFT

TRANSPORT
L-760

IDENTIFICATION OF SOVIET-RUSSIAN AIRCRAFT

RUSSIAN
ARMY

TRANSPORT-BOMBER TB-1

Monoplane—medium bomber—used for freight and parachute troops.

Crew:	Five or six.
Armament:	Three machine guns, flexible.
Ammunition:	
Bomb load:	1,764 pounds, normal.
Radio:	
Armor:	
Motors:	Two 680 horsepower M17 (BMW VI).
Maximum speed:	128 miles per hour.
Rate of climb:	9,840 feet in 15 minutes.
Service ceiling:	16,400 feet.
Maximum range:	620 miles.
Wing span:	

IDENTIFICATION OF SOVIET-RUSSIAN AIRCRAFT

TRANSPORT-BOMBER TB-1

IDENTIFICATION OF SOVIET-RUSSIAN AIRCRAFT

RUSSIAN ARMY

TRANSPORT-BOMBER TB-3

Slightly swept-back, slightly tapered, square tip, midwing cabin monoplane, four motors, fixed landing gear, used as bomber-transport, long blunt nose, may be with different types depending upon mission of airplane. Antiquated as bomber, still used as transport plane and for parachute and air-borne Infantry.

Crew:	Nine or 12.
Armament:	Three flexible machine guns.
Ammunition:	
Bomb load:	4,400 pounds, normal; 8,800 pounds, maximum; or 24 air-borne troops.
Radio:	
Armor:	
Motors:	Four M17, 600 horsepower at 328 feet or M34, 850 horsepower at 328 feet.
Maximum speed:	113 miles at 328 feet or 138 miles at 6,650 feet.
Rate of climb:	9,840 feet in 46 minutes or 6,650 feet in 15 minutes.
Service ceiling:	16,000 feet.
Maximum range:	875 miles, normal; 1,875 miles, maximum.
Wing span:	

TRANSPORT-BOMBER TB-3

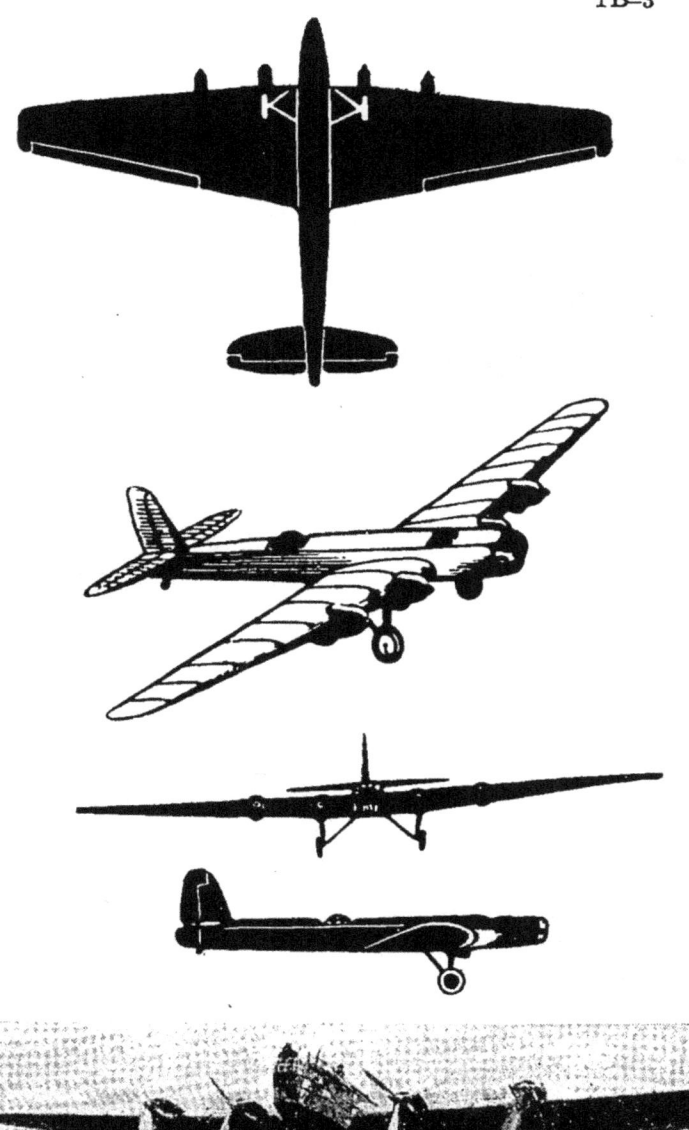

IDENTIFICATION OF SOVIET-RUSSIAN AIRCRAFT

RUSSIAN
ARMY

TRAINING U-2

Straight, round tip, biplane, open cockpit, fixed landing gear, used as training-practice-liaison and hospital airplane.

Crew: Two.
Armament:
Ammunition:
Bomb load:
Radio:
Armor:
Motors: One M11, 110 horsepower.
Maximum speed: 93 miles at 328 feet.
Rate of climb:
Service ceiling: 14,760 feet.
Maximum range: 250 miles.
Wing span:

IDENTIFICATION OF SOVIET-RUSSIAN AIRCRAFT

TRAINING
U-2

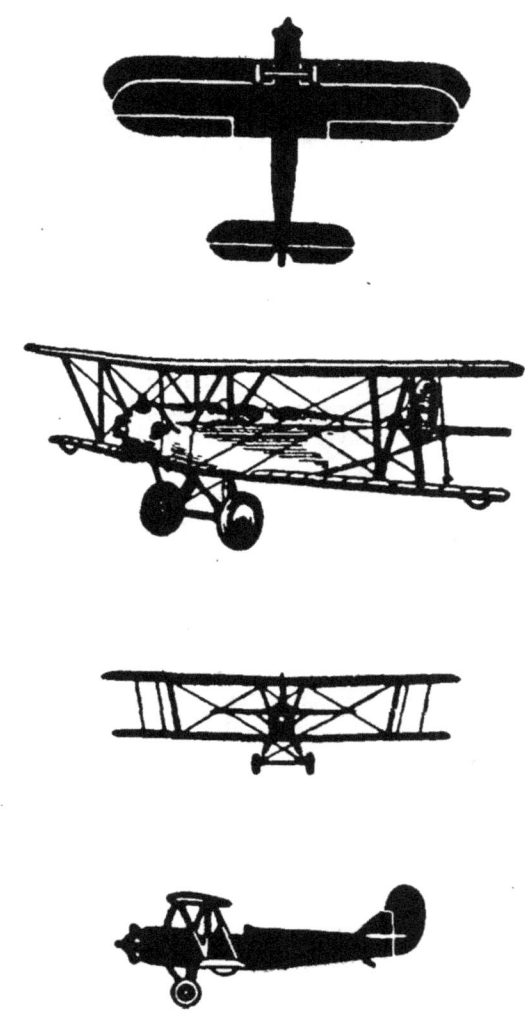

RUSSIAN ARMY

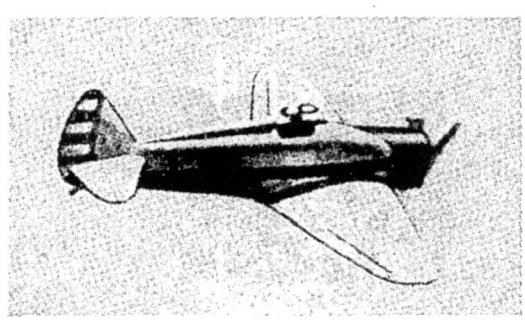

TRAINING-LIAISON UT-1

Slightly swept-back, slightly tapered, elliptical, single motor, low-wing monoplane, open cockpit, fixed landing gear, used as training-practice and liaison airplane; also on pontoons.

Crew: One.
Armament:
Ammunition:
Bomb load:
Radio:
Armor:
Motors: One M1, 120 horsepower.
Maximum speed: 120 miles per hour.
Rate of speed:
Service ceiling:
Maximum range:
Wing span:

IDENTIFICATION OF SOVIET-RUSSIAN AIRCRAFT

TRAINING-LIAISON
UT-1

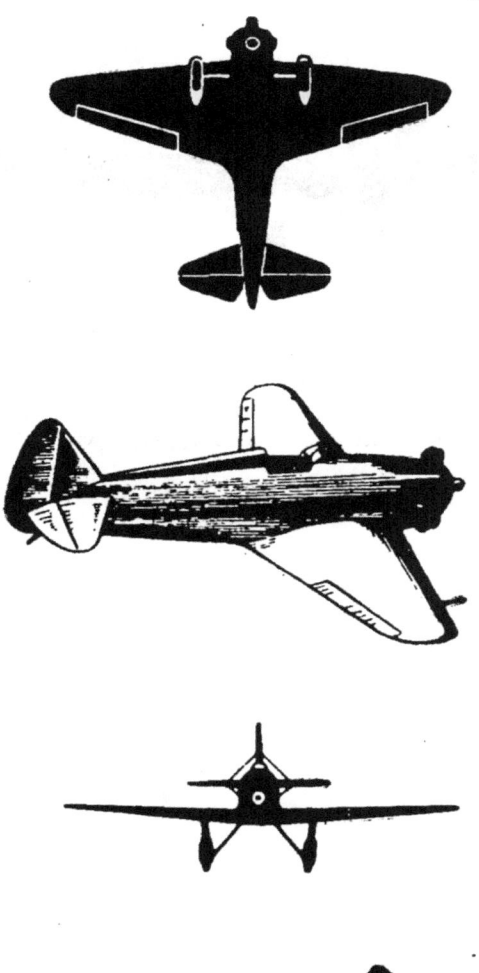

IDENTIFICATION OF SOVIET-RUSSIAN AIRCRAFT

RUSSIAN ARMY

TRAINING-LIAISON UT-2

Slightly tapered, round tip, low-wing, single motor, monoplane, open cockpit, fixed landing gear, used as training-practice and liaison airplane; also appears with motors.

Crew: Two.
Armament:
Ammunition:
Bomb load:
Radio:
Armor:
Motors: One M11, 100 horsepower.
Maximum speed: 120 miles per hour.
Rate of climb:
Service ceiling:
Maximum range:
Wing span:

IDENTIFICATION OF SOVIET-RUSSIAN AIRCRAFT

TRAINING-LIAISON
UT-2

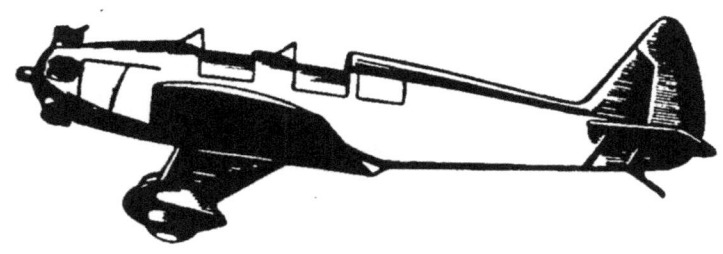

IDENTIFICATION OF SOVIET-RUSSIAN AIRCRAFT

RUSSIAN ARMY

PRACTICE-PURSUIT I-5

Antiquated single seater, practice pursuit airplane, straight, round tip, biplane, open cockpit, fixed landing gear.

Crew: One.
Armament: Two fixed machine guns.
Ammunition:
Bomb load: 110 pounds.
Radio:
Armor:
Motors: One M22, 450 horsepower.
Maximum speed: 172 miles at 328 feet.
Rate of climb: 9,840 feet in 3.8 minutes.
Service ceiling. 19,700 feet.
Maximum range: 372 miles or 2½ hours.
Wing span:

IDENTIFICATION OF SOVIET-RUSSIAN AIRCRAFT

PRACTICE-PURSUIT
I-5

NAVAL AIRCRAFT

RUSSIAN
NAVY

FIGHTER SEAPLANE

Straight leading edge, swept-back rounded trailing edge, round tip, twin floats, seaplane, single motor, inclosed cockpit.

Crew: One.
Armament: Two machine guns.
Ammunition:
Bomb load:
Radio:
Armor:
Motors: One 680 horsepower M17 (BMW VI).
Maximum speed: 149 miles per hour.
Rate of climb: 16,400 feet in 8.5 minutes.
Service ceiling: 23,950 feet.
Maximum range: 310 miles.
Wing span:

IDENTIFICATION OF SOVIET-RUSSIAN AIRCRAFT

FIGHTER
SEAPLANE

RUSSIAN
NAVY

FIGHTER SEVERSKY

Two-seater, fighter, amphibian.

Crew:
Armament:
Ammunition:
Bomb load:
Radio:
Armor:
Motors:
Maximum speed:
Rate of climb:
Service ceiling:
Maximum range:
Wing span: 36 feet.

FIGHTER
SEVERSKY

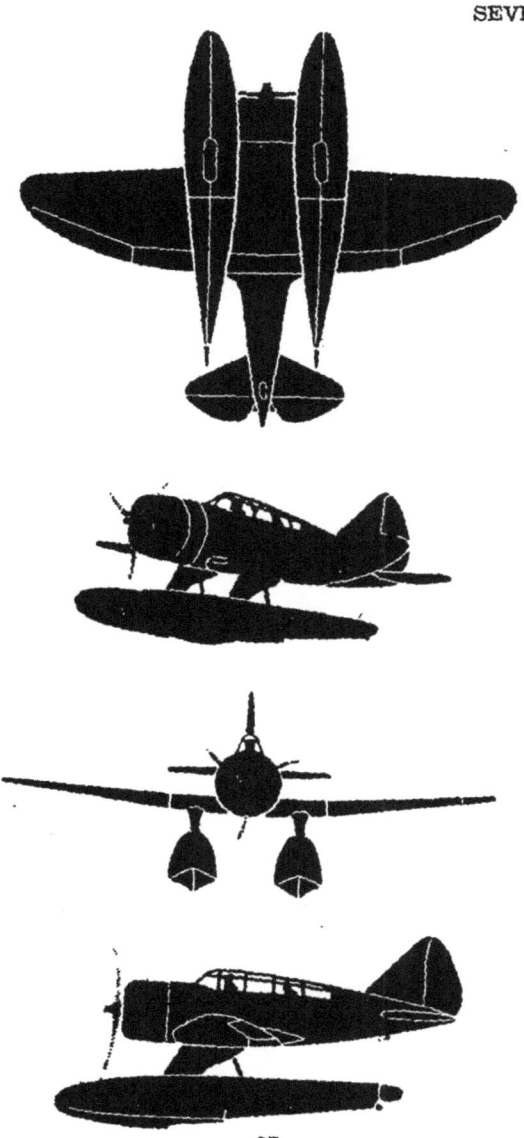

IDENTIFICATION OF SOVIET-RUSSIAN AIRCRAFT

RUSSIAN NAVY

TORPEDO-BOMBER (SEAPLANE MTB-1)

Floating version of TB-3.

Crew: Five or six.
Armament: Three flexible machine guns.
Ammunition:
Bomb load: Alternate bomb or torpedo (880 pounds).
Radio:
Armor:
Motors: Two 680 horsepower M17 (BMW VI).
Maximum speed: 124 miles per hour.
Rate of climb:
Service ceiling:
Maximum range: 594 miles or 6 hours.
Wing span:

IDENTIFICATION OF SOVIET-RUSSIAN AIRCRAFT

TORPEDO-BOMBER
(SEAPLANE MTB-1)

IDENTIFICATION OF SOVIET-RUSSIAN AIRCRAFT

RUSSIAN
NAVY

RECONNAISSANCE MBR-2

Straight, square, monoplane, flying boat, pointed tail fin, motor mounted separately above wing, fixed wing floats, long pointed nose.

Crew:	Three or four.
Armament:	Four 7.62 Shkaas machine guns, flexible.
Ammunition:	
Bomb load:	440 pounds.
Radio:	Wireless.
Armor:	
Motors:	One M17, 600 to 680 horsepower.
Maximum speed:	136 miles per hour.
Rate of climb:	3,280 feet in 3.5 minutes; 9,280 feet in 13 minutes.
Service ceiling:	17,400 feet.
Maximum range:	596 to 745 miles.
Wing span:	44 feet.

IDENTIFICATION OF SOVIET-RUSSIAN AIRCRAFT

RECONNAISSANCE
MBR-2

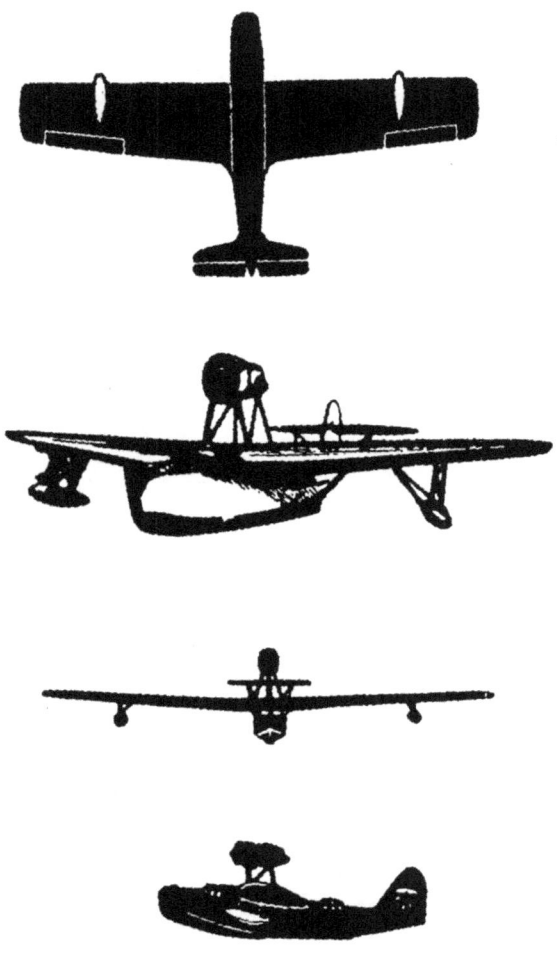

IDENTIFICATION OF SOVIET-RUSSIAN AIRCRAFT

RUSSIAN
NAVY

RECONNAISSANCE MBR-4

Crew: Three.
Armament: Two flexible machine guns.
Ammunition:
Bomb load:
Radio:
Armor:
Motors: One M17, 600 horsepower at 6,560 feet.
Maximum speed: 138 miles at 6,560 feet.
Rate of climb: 9,840 feet in 20 minutes.
Service ceiling: 14,760 feet.
Maximum range: 625 miles without bombs.
Wing span: 54 feet.

IDENTIFICATION OF SOVIET-RUSSIAN AIRCRAFT

RECONNAISSANCE
MBR-4

RUSSIAN
NAVY

COASTAL RECONNAISSANCE MBR-5

Slightly dihedral, monoplane, flying boat, pusher type, floats attached to under surface of wings.

Crew:
Armament:
Ammunition:
Bomb load:
Radio:
Armor:
Motors:
Maximum speed:
Rate of climb:
Service ceiling:
Maximum range:
Wing span:

IDENTIFICATION OF SOVIET-RUSSIAN AIRCRAFT

COASTAL RECONNAISSANCE MBR–5

**RUSSIAN
NAVY**

SHIP PLANE KOR-1

Straight, round tip, biplane, single float seaplane, single motor, closed cockpit, floats attached to under surface of wings near wing tips.

Crew:
Armament:
Ammunition:
Bomb load:
Radio:
Armor:
Motors:
Maximum speed:
Rate of climb:
Service ceiling:
Maximum range:
Wing span:

IDENTIFICATION OF SOVIET-RUSSIAN AIRCRAFT

**SHIP PLANE
KOR-1**

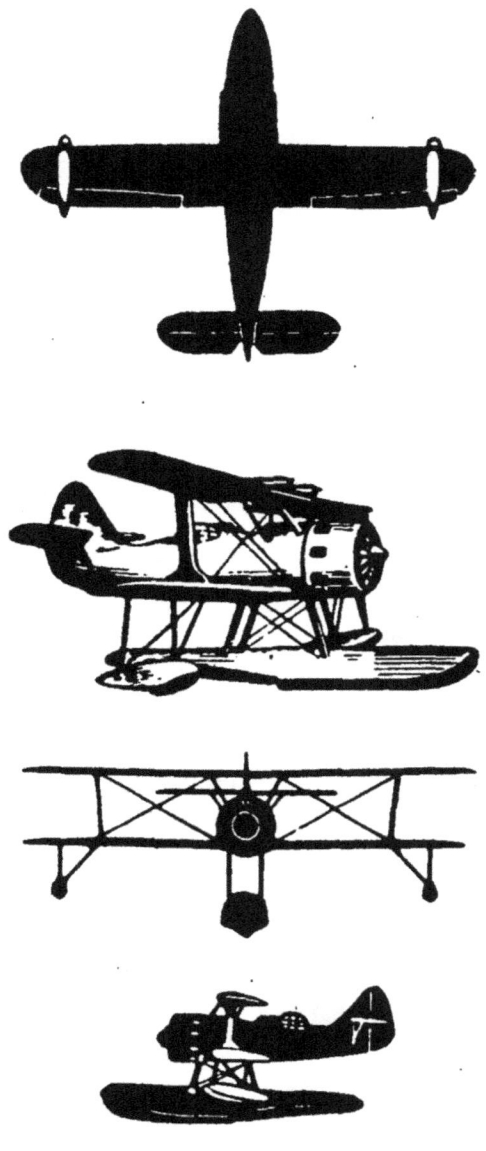

IDENTIFICATION OF SOVIET-RUSSIAN AIRCRAFT

RUSSIAN
NAVY

RECONNAISSANCE FLYING BOAT MDR-5

Five-seat, twin-engined, reconnaissance flying boat.

Crew: Five.
Armament: Three machine-gun positions.
Ammunition:
Bomb load:
Radio:
Armor:
Motors: Two 680 horsepower M17 (BMW VI).
Maximum speed: 135 miles per hour.
Rate of climb: 9,840 feet in 16 minutes.
Service ceiling: 16,400 feet.
Maximum range: 900 miles.
Wing span:

IDENTIFICATION OF SOVIET-RUSSIAN AIRCRAFT

RECONNAISSANCE FLYING BOAT
MDR–5

RUSSIAN
NAVY

RECONNAISSANCE FLYING BOAT MR-5

Obsolescent.

Crew: Three.
Armament: Two machine guns.
Ammunition:
Bomb load:
Radio:
Armor:
Motors: One 680 horsepower M17 (BMW VI).
Maximum speed: 140 miles per hour.
Rate of climb: 9,840 feet in 12.5 minutes.
Service ceiling: 17,050 feet.
Maximum range: 620 miles.
Wing span:

IDENTIFICATION OF SOVIET-RUSSIAN AIRCRAFT

RECONNAISSANCE FLYING BOAT
MR–5

IDENTIFICATION OF SOVIET-RUSSIAN AIRCRAFT

RUSSIAN
NAVY

SAVOIA 55 RECONNAISSANCE (OR BOMBER)

Slightly dihedral, swept-back, slightly tapered, round tip, monoplane, twin boat seaplane, twin motors in tandem, inclosed cabin, spar fuselage.

Crew:
Armament:
Ammunition:
Bomb load:
Radio:
Armor:
Motors:
Maximum speed:
Rate of climb:
Service ceiling:
Maximum range:
Wing span: 80 feet.

IDENTIFICATION OF SOVIET-RUSSIAN AIRCRAFT

SAVOIA 55 RECONNAISSANCE (OR BOMBER)

IDENTIFICATION OF SOVIET-RUSSIAN AIRCRAFT

RUSSIAN
NAVY

COASTAL RECONNAISSANCE A. N. T. 22

Monoplane with twin flying boats, three twin motors each in tandem.

Crew:
Armament:
Ammunition:
Bomb load: 22,000 pounds.
Radio:
Armor:
Motors: Six 800 horsepower M34, mounted above wings in three tandem pairs.
Maximum speed:
Rate of climb:
Service ceiling: 6,300 feet.
Maximum range:
Wing span:

IDENTIFICATION OF SOVIET-RUSSIAN AIRCRAFT

COASTAL RECONNAISSANCE
A. N. T. 22

www.ingramcontent.com/pod-product-compliance
Lightning Source LLC
Chambersburg PA
CBHW061453040426
42450CB00007B/1338